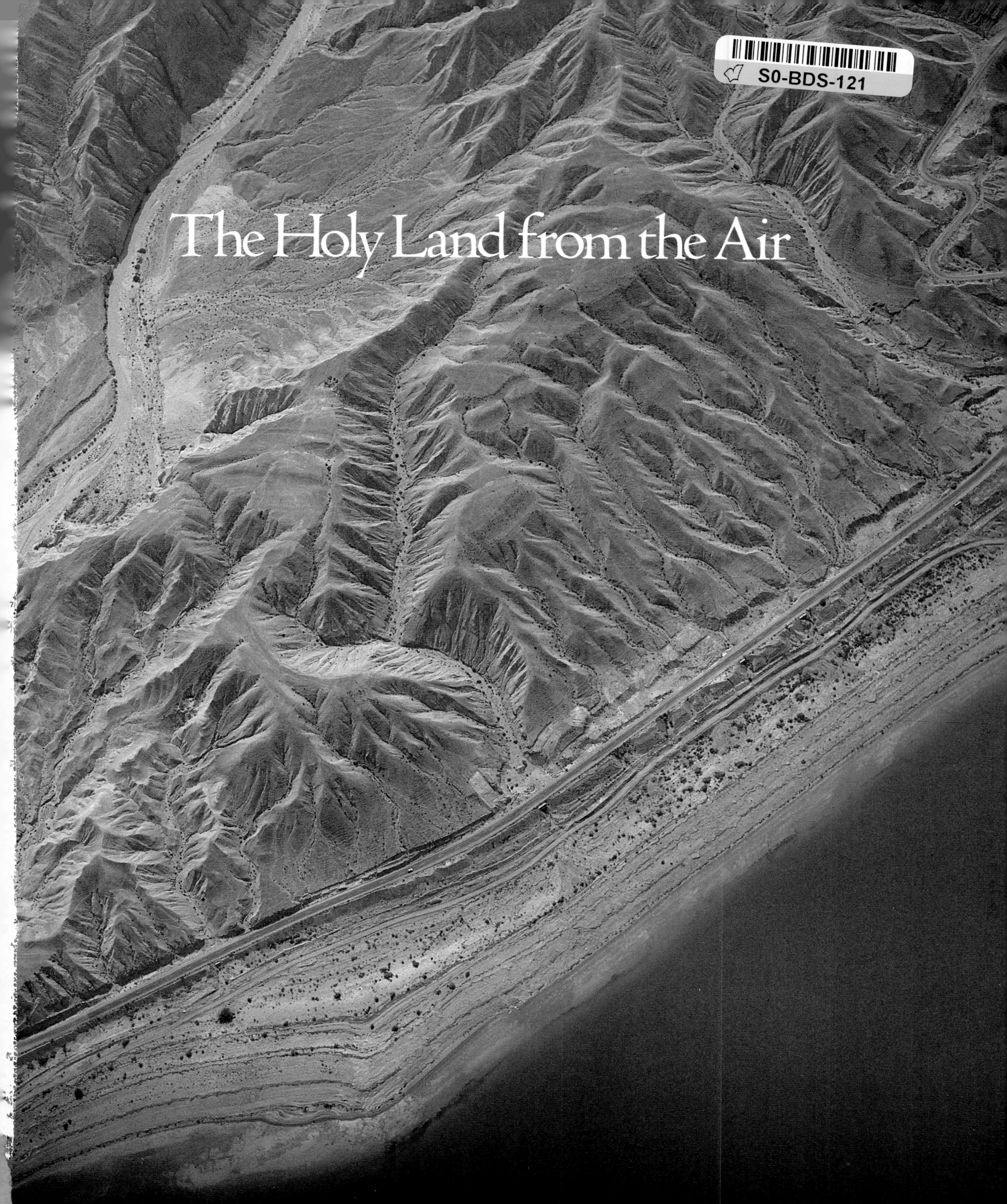

The Holy Land from the Air

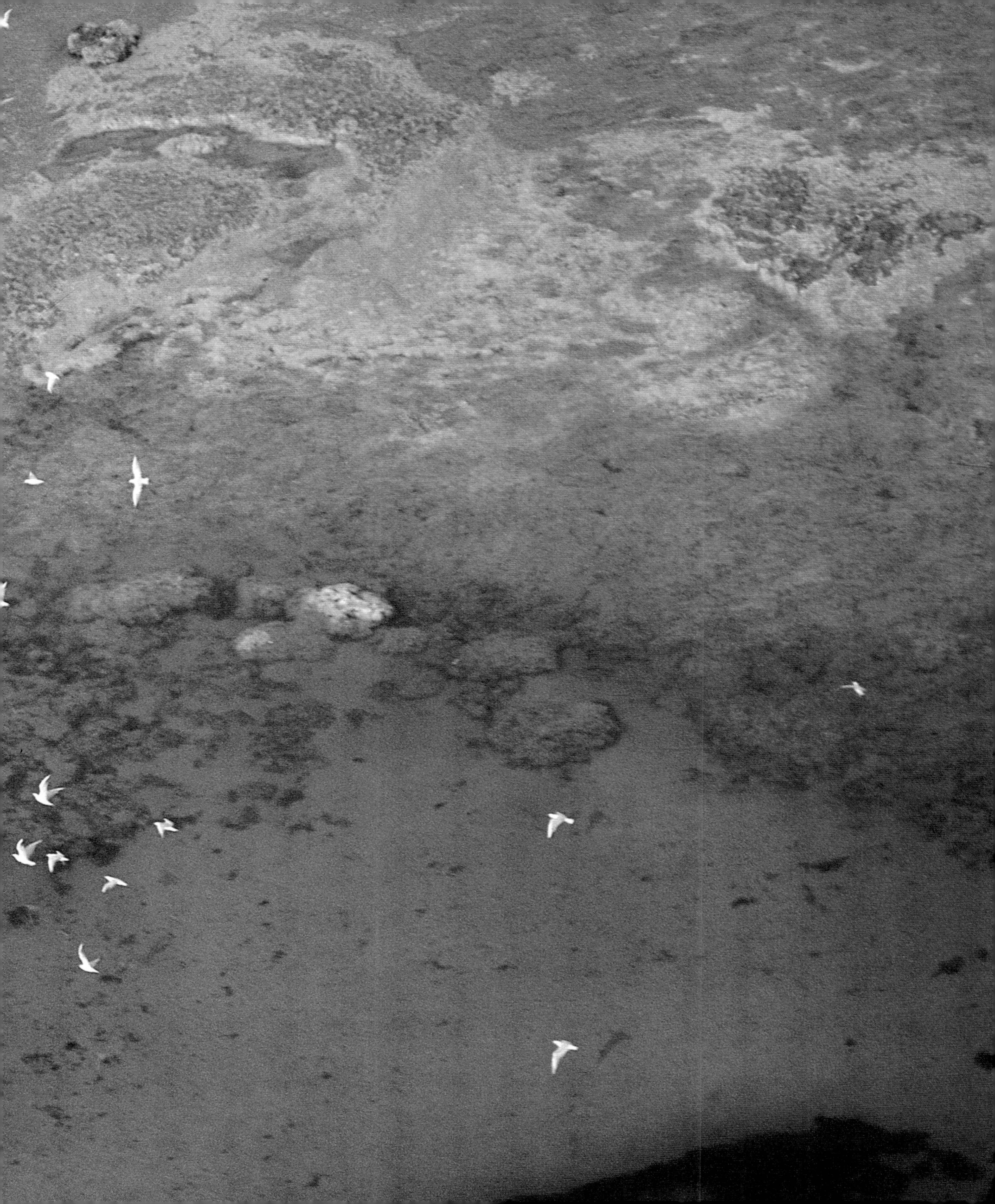

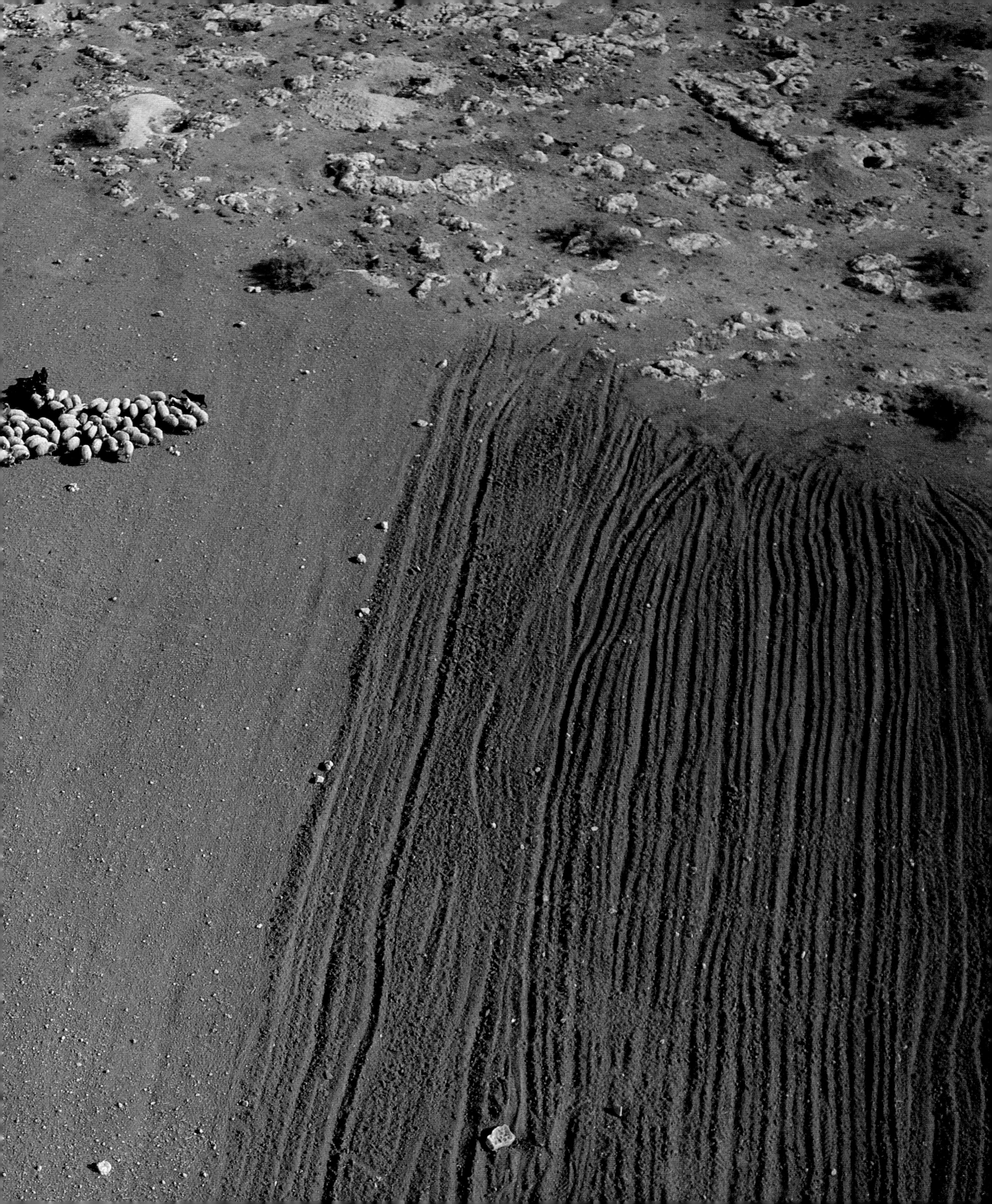

The Holy Land from the Air

Text by Amos Elon
Photographs by Richard Nowitz

Harry N. Abrams, Inc., Publishers, New York
in association with The Domino Press, Jerusalem

Editor: Beverly Fazio
Designer: Michael Hentges

The publishers gratefully acknowledge the contribution of Delta, distributors of Kodak in Israel

Library of Congress
Cataloging-in-Publication Data

Elon, Amos.
The Holy Land from the air.

1. Israel—Description and travel—Views.
2. Israel—Aerial photographs. 3. Israel.
I. Nowitz, Richard. II. Title.
DS108.5.E625 1987 915.69 87–1390
ISBN 0–8109–1164–7

Published in 1987 by Harry N. Abrams, Incorporated, New York, and The Domino Press Limited, Jerusalem.

Times Mirror Books

Printed and bound by Amilcare Pizzi S.p.A., Milan

PAGE 1: The wilderness of Judea meets the Dead Sea—at more than 1,300 feet below sea level, the lowest spot on earth—a few miles south of Qumran.

PAGES 2–3: Birds in flight over the Mediterranean Sea, south of Athlit.

PAGES 4–5: Flocks of sheep at Wadi Farah, in the Judean Desert.

PAGES 6–7: In the hills of Samaria, carefully terraced land. Some of the stone walls that protect the rich, brown soil from erosion date from biblical times.

PAGE 8: At Beth Shearim, near the western corner of the Esdralon Valley, a vast network of catacombs with more than four hundred magnificent, ornate tombs forms a unique monument to Jewish material culture under Roman and Byzantine rule. Rabi Judah ha-Nasi, the compiler of the *Mishna*, is among those buried here: "Miracles were wrought on that day. It was evening and all the towns gathered to mourn him. Eighteen synagogues praised him and bore him to Beth Shearim" (Ketubot 12:35a). The entrance to the necropolis is seen at the center of this picture. The necropolis is today part of a national park.

Contents

Introduction

Between the river Jordan and the eastern shore of the Mediterranean Sea—along some two hundred miles of the latter—there stretches a narrow, relatively small country, very poorly endowed by nature, which yet, as the land of Israel, as the Holy Land, or as Palestine, figures in the consciousness of millions unlike any other place on earth.

The nerves of three great religions quiver in its dry, dusty soil. Human history in this country extends over half a million years and is more complex here than elsewhere. This narrow landbridge between continents has seen more peoples, cultures, faiths, languages—and invading armies—move back and forth across it continually than anywhere on earth.

Too much time has been poured into too narrow a space. The passenger in a low-flying airplane coming in from Europe over the sea, at about 34 40′ E., 32 10′ N., notices at first a dull film of mist rising over the horizon, next a low, almost straight line of yellow-brownish shore, shimmering in the sun. It is not by any means an inviting coast. There are no offshore islands nor any deep estuaries or fully sheltered gulfs. There is barely a break in the long line of foam where land and sea meet. Below there is still the great semicircle of the sea, green when looked at in the morning but mauve or purple in the afternoon, and, with the sun behind you, almost "wine-colored," as was Homer's fabled sea around the isles of Greece.

The plane crosses low, over the white beach. Almost instantly the view of the sea is lost. The light is harsh, and the first houses come into view, with their flat roofs, densely clustered between the dusty trees, the crowded highways, the chimneys, the bare dunes, and the powerlines. Orange groves fan out in broad green patches to the foothills farther east.

The view is barer than an American or European eye might desire, but it is softened by the haze the heat sheds over all. The maritime plain, a narrow strip of greens and browns and yellows, runs north and south between the mountains and the sea. This was once the ancient land of the Philistines and a famous warpath between empires, from Ramses and Nebuchadnezzar to Alexander the Great, Pompey, Titus, Godfrey, Saladin, and Napoleon. Nebuchadnezzar marched his army down the plain toward Jerusalem and Egypt; Napoleon, with his ambition à la Alexander of an empire in the East, marched his army up the same plain from Egypt to his first great defeat in Acre, at the hands of Sir Sidney Smith, of whom he later at St. Helena said bitterly, "That man made me miss my destiny." Monotonously they have all followed the same great highway, picked up the same pestilence in the same marsh, and fought their crucial battles in the same natural theater, the plain's gateway to Damascus at Megiddo, also known as Armageddon. There the greatest battle of all—the Apocalypse, when the Kings of the Earth and of the whole world are to be destroyed—was placed almost routinely by the zealots who imagined it.

More than thirty centuries have left an imprint in this narrow plain. Canaanites and Egyptians have passed through it, as have Assyrians, Philistines, Hittites, Hebrews, Greeks,

Ptolemies, Seleucids and Phoenicians, Romans, Parthians, Persians, Byzantines, Arabs, French, German, and Italian Crusaders, Saracens and Kurds, Mamluks, English colonialists, modern Palestinian Arabs, and Jews. In the eleventh century, when the Crusaders first reached this coast, it was still covered, as it had been since the time of the Hebrew kings, by a great forest of oak trees—Tasso's "enchanted grove." Later the trees disappeared almost entirely and the plain turned into swamp and moor, a silent, mournful expanse ravaged by centuries of warfare, fever, piracy, and neglect. This was how the first modern Jewish settlers found it in the early 1880s. Its ancient towns, which in antiquity had held over a million inhabitants, lay in ruins, buried under the wandering dunes. The dry land was rich enough but given over to weeds. A few years later, in 1905, a twenty-year-old Jewish pioneer named David Ben-Gurion, the future prime minister of Israel, disembarked at Jaffa. At that time Jaffa was a squalid cluster of houses built of mud and porous sandstone, the accumulated debris of innumerable previous civilizations. Ben-Gurion walked through the squalor and the nearby swamp, contracted malaria, hired himself out as a farm worker, and wrote to his father in Czarist-controlled Plonsk, Poland: "Who is to complain, to sigh, to despair? In twenty years our country will be one of the most blooming, most beautiful and happiest; an old-new nation will florish in an ancient-new land."

Today the restored lanes and stairways around the old port of Jaffa constitute a picturesque quarter of Tel Aviv, the modern town that began as a garden suburb of old Jaffa in 1908. The coastal plain is now the most densely populated, the most urbanized and industrialized region of Israel. As the airplane flies east across the plain, directly on the left is the great metropolitan area of Tel Aviv. Here over half of Israel's population of four million live and work. From the air the city is a sea of asphalt roofs, solar heating panels, and television aerials. High-rise buildings sprout in the business center and on the teeming beach. To the north are yellow dunes and orange groves, interspersed by smaller towns and villages, up to the ancient Roman port of Caesarea and the modern city of Haifa. On a clear day you can see almost the entire country from the airplane. You see the Carmel mountain range, which begins seventy miles away and at its northernmost tip touches the sea. Still farther north is the old Crusader port of St. Jean d'Acre. Only a few decades ago five or six rivers—among them the torrent Kishon—still crossed the narrow plain from the mountains to the sea, as in Judges 5:21: "The river of Kishon swept them away, that ancient river, the river of Kishon." Of those only two or three are left nowadays, polluted by industrial wastes or tapped off to serve a new national water grid pumping water from the relatively fertile north and center to the arid south. Looking down and right now, to the south, you see still more modern housing developments, dunes, orange groves, vineyards, and industrial parks. A crowded superhighway runs down toward the Egyptian frontier. The new port city of Ashdod, founded on the dunes in the 1950s, is clearly visible. So, on a clear day, is Ashkelon, another modern city farther south along the seashore, built on the site of an ancient Egyptian citadel of the nineteenth century B.C. The reconquest of Ashkelon, by Rameses II in the thirteenth century B.C., shortly before the exodus of the Hebrews, is recorded on a wall of the temple of Amon at Luxor in upper Egypt ("Canaan pillaged . . . Askelon taken"). The city appears later in David's famous lament for Jonathan: "Tell it not in Gath, publish it not in the streets of Askelon; lest the daughters of the Philistines rejoice" (2 Samuel 1:20). As you fly over Ashkelon, its pretty, whitewashed houses glitter in the sun; so too do those of Ashdod, and also the massive laboratories, office buildings, and dormitories of the nearby Weizmann Institute of Science, all enclosed in a magnificent park. It is always astounding in this dry land, where plants must be carefully tended and artificially irrigated for nine months of the year, to see such large areas of well-tended lawn.

Farther east, toward the mountains, the scenery quickly changes. There are vineyards and orchards and plowed cotton fields. Huge sprinklers turn, irrigating the crops, and dust-croppers fly in low to spray them. Where the cotton fields reach the foothills of Judea the rocks seem at first bare. As the plane flies nearer, you see the thick brush and scrub and almonds and pines and cypress trees that dot the stony, deep brown earth. Between the shoulders of the mountains is the dull green mass of olive groves. It is a parched and broken land of crags and lonely windswept pines and old Arab villages with famous (Hebrew) biblical names etched in concentric circles into stony hilltops. From the airplane the carefully terraced dark brown land resembles seasoned polished wood.

The villages are of a singular beauty. Their little stone houses fit into the dry mountainside like teeth into a jawbone. There is a merciless clarity here in the sunlit mountain air. The clouds hang stagnant in the sky; their shadows crouch below and cast fantastic shapes on the rugged earth. The sky is luminous, except when shaded by winter rains. At night enormous stars hang in the fragrant darkness like great chandeliers.

The ancient Hebrews were a highland people, and it was from these hills, the "high-places of Israel," that they looked down upon the seaborn invaders from the west, the Philistines and the technologically superior Roman armies, just as in our own century the Palestinian Arabs poised upon these same historic hills looked down upon (and opposed with as much zeal and with as little success) the recent return of the Jews. From the mountaintops, toward the plain, there is a good view of the sea. Settling in the Judean hills in the fourth century, Saint Jerome, used to the vast expanses of the Roman Empire, confessed his astonishment at the short distance from Bethlehem to the Mediterranean Sea—a matter of only a few leagues—and ever since, travelers have been struck by, and remarked on, the close proximity of the well-known legendary and historical sites. What a small country this is, you want to exclaim. And yet a certain sense of spaciousness is enhanced by the stupendous contrast of desert with fertility and by the drama of a landscape bordered on the one hand by the inhospitable sea and on the other by the rough wall of mountains. The mountains rise rugged in the east. The mountains for untold millions of believers have been and still are a landscape of the mind as well: the very heart of the Holy Land, even though, as an eighteenth-century English pilgrim wrote, "Terra sancta being the name only, for all holiness is banished therefrom," by its brutal history and its perpetual disorder. Only a few decades ago the hill country still seemed physically unchanged from the days of Gideon, Saul, or David. Here, according to the Bible, Joshua called upon the sun to lengthen the day of battle and Deborah sang her savage song of victory over Sisra. Here the Canaanites offered human sacrifice to Moloch. Through these same hills Jesus walked with his disciples and promised the kingdom of heaven to all who are wretched and poor, and the prophet who was "among the herdsmen of Tekoah" proclaimed his message of universal peace and justice. Here, according to the Bible, Jacob wrestled with the angel and "called the name of the place Peniel [God's countenance]," saying " 'for I have seen God face to face' " (Genesis 32:30); and here the young David slew Goliath with his shepherd's sling and a stone. In the Vale of Elah, where, the Bible tells us this last event took place, the huge dish antenna of a satellite tracking station overwhelms the immediate scene, but a few hundred feet up the steep hill the landscape once again looks as it must have in the Bronze Age, three or three and a half thousand years ago. A few ilex trees, the large robust evergreens that gave the place its name (*elah* is Hebrew for ilex tree), are still about. The vale is the gateway from the Philistine plain to the Judean hills, and the shepherd boy from Bethlehem who the Bible says was sent by his father for news of the battle would only have had to run about ten miles from his father's house to the site of his encounter with Goliath.

In another direction, about the same distance away, we reach Sha'ar Hagai (Gate of the Valley), the traditional pilgrim route from the coast to Jerusalem, and the route of many an army as well. Like all other access routes to Jerusalem from the west and the east, it is a narrow mountain pass, the edges steep and often precipitous. The springs lie few and far apart—a land of ambushes and entanglements where everything conspires to give to the few easy means of defense against the many. From the air you look down on extensive afforestation projects of the last fifty years and the broad, six-lane highway that has been cut rather brutally through the limestone rocks. (A mysterious tree disease that felled large tracts of forest in recent years is often ascribed to the road.) The highway climbs from the Emmaus of the Gospels, where the risen Jesus broke bread with the disciples, and up the road to Abu Ghosh, the biblical Beit Ye'arim, where in the nineteenth century a local Bedouin chieftain still levied tolls on all pilgrims to Jerusalem. To Beit Ye'arim, the Bible tells us, the ark of the covenant was brought back by the victorious Hebrews after it was recovered from the Philistines. Here the prophet judge Samuel again urged them to put away the effigies and strange gods and to worship the true god only. The admonition (it was apparently not very much heeded, for the tribes kept their tutelary deities much as Italian peasants hold on to their local Madonnas) is commemorated by the monumental church of Our Lady of the Ark of the Covenant in today's Abu Ghosh. Farther up the mountain on the right lie the ruins of Al Qastal (with a new village at its feet), which took its name from the Castellum that guarded the highway in Roman days; and on the left is the high hill that overlooks Jerusalem from the northwest.

From here, finally, the city can be seen with the naked eye. Here the pilgrims and the generals in command of invading armies have traditionally paused to behold, piously or covetously, the famous city of their quest, dark against the morning sun, with its ramparts, its gilded domes, its palaces and houses of worship. The Crusaders knelt at this observation point and called it Mont Joye. Jewish pilgrims poised here for a first look at the city and traditionally rent their garments in mourning for its ruins. That first view of the city is as stunning today as it must have been when three thousand years ago the first pilgrims arrived to worship at the first great temple of Solomon, on Mount Moriah, an acropolis above the city. On Moriah, Abraham, according to the legend, made ready to sacrifice Isaac, and, a

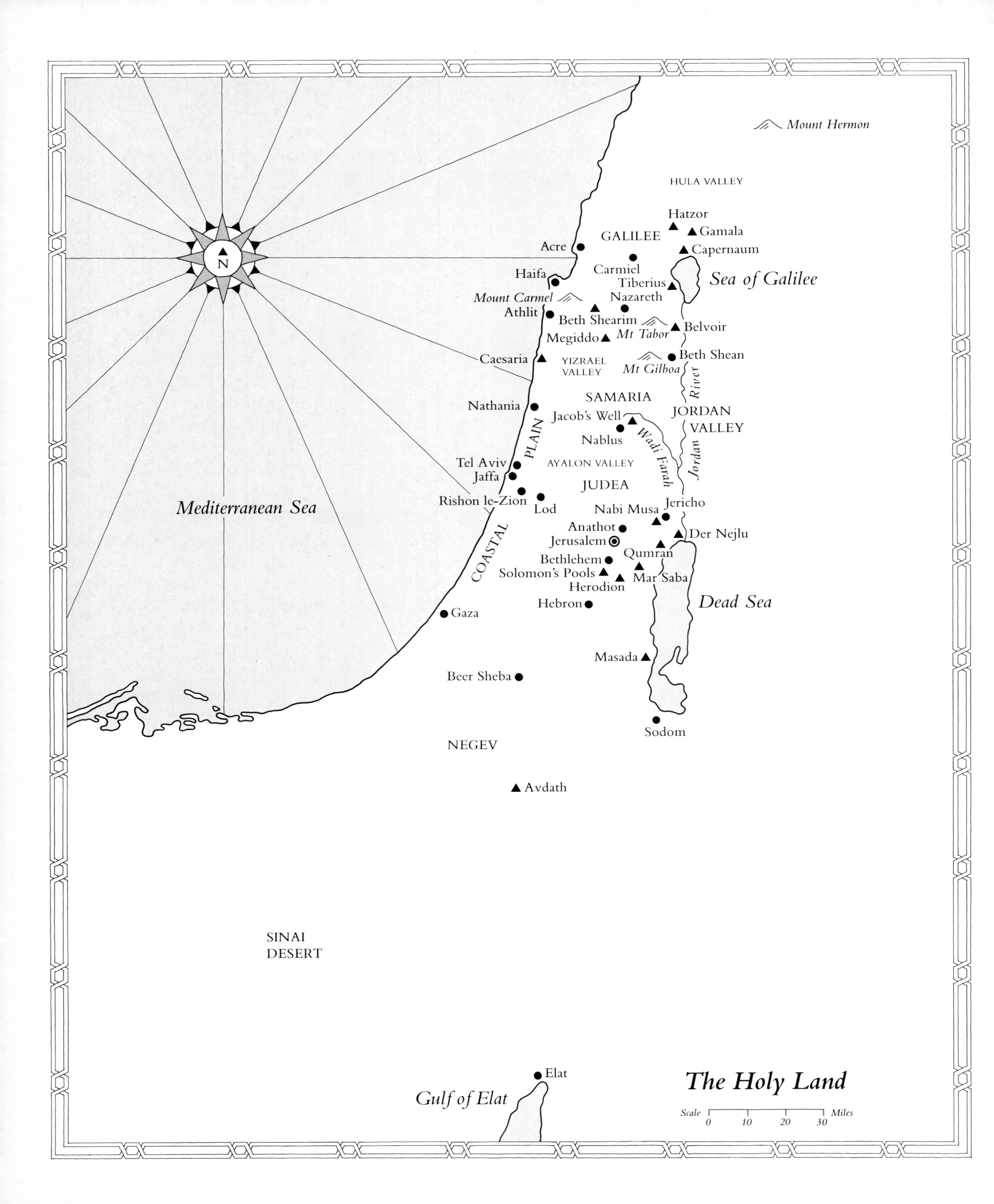
The Holy Land
Mount Hermon
HULA VALLEY
Hatzor
Gamala
GALILEE
Acre
Capernaum
Carmiel
Haifa
Tiberius
Sea of Galilee
Mount Carmel
Nazareth
Athlit
Beth Shearim
Belvoir
Megiddo
Mt Tabor
Beth Shean
Caesaria
YIZRAEL VALLEY
Mt Gilboa
River
SAMARIA
Nathania
JORDAN
Jacob's Well
VALLEY
Nablus
Wadi Farah
Jordan
PLAIN
Tel Aviv
AYALON VALLEY
Jaffa
JUDEA
Rishon le-Zion
Lod
Jericho
Nabi Musa
Mediterranean Sea
Anathot
Der Nejlu
Jerusalem
Qumran
COASTAL
Bethlehem
Solomon's Pools
Mar Saba
Herodion
Dead Sea
Hebron
Gaza
Masada
Beer Sheba
Sodom
NEGEV
Avdath
SINAI DESERT
Elat
Gulf of Elat
N
Scale 0 10 20 30 Miles

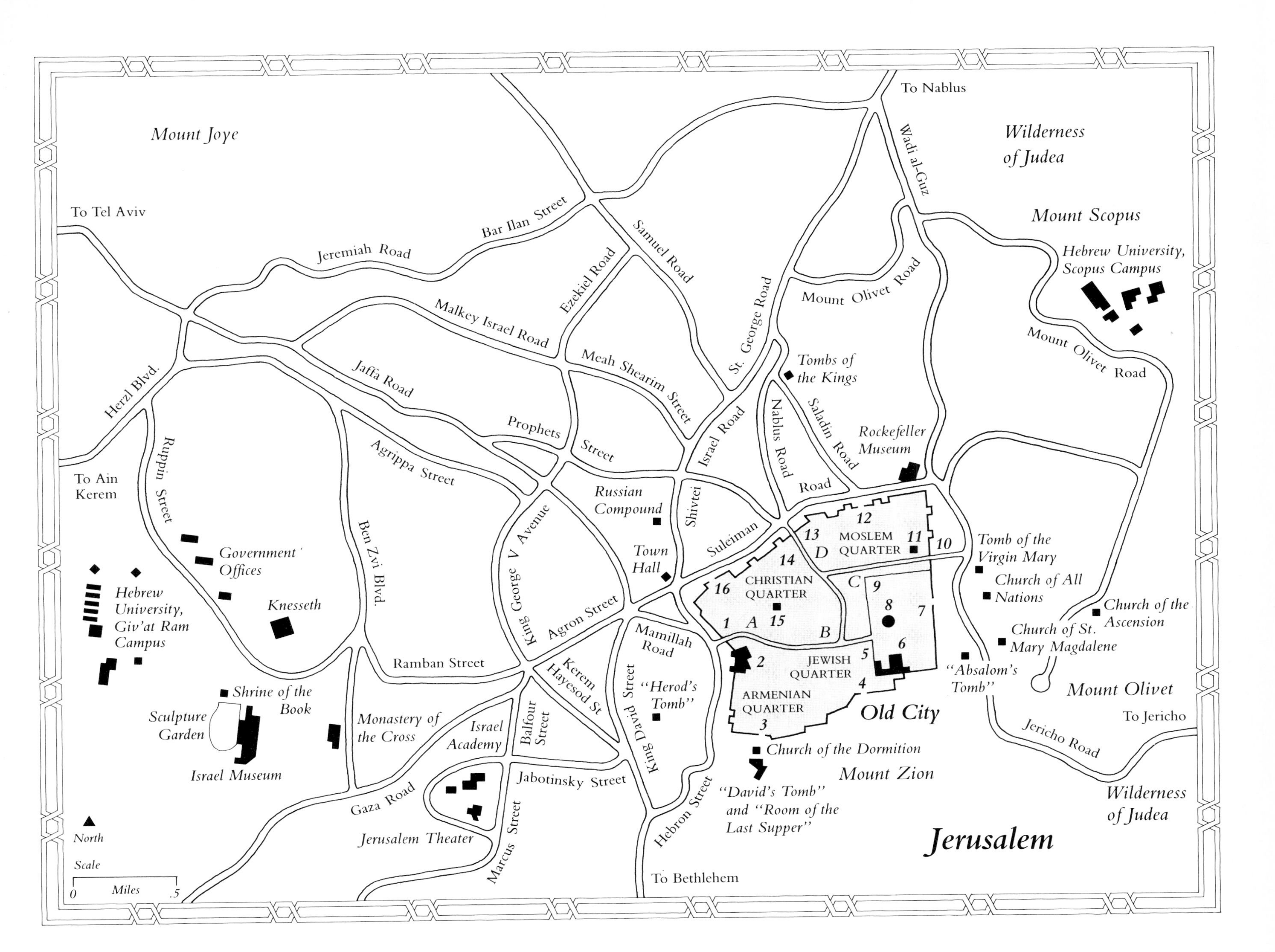

Jerusalem Map Legend

1 *Jaffa Gate*	7 *Golden Gate*	13 *Damascus Gate*	A *David Street*
2 *Citadel of David*	8 *Dome of the Rock*	14 *"Solomon's Quarries"*	B *Chain Street*
3 *Zion Gate*	9 *Antonia Fortress*	15 *Basilica of the Holy Sepulchre*	C *Via Dolorosa*
4 *Dung Gate*	10 *St. Stephen's Gate*	16 *New Gate*	D *Al Wad Road*
5 *Western Wall*	11 *St. Anne Church*		
6 *El-Aqsa Mosque*	12 *Herod's Gate*		

The Holy Land Map Legend

● *Cities*

▲ *Archaeological Sites*

Mountains

millennium after Solomon, Herod built his great temple, which the future Roman emperor Titus would later destroy. Under Hadrian (who destroyed Jerusalem once again and forbade the Jews to approach it) the Romans worshiped a great statue of Jupiter on Moriah, which Constantine, the first Christian emperor, demolished. The Moslems later built on Moriah two magnificent mosques, which the Crusaders turned into churches and the Moslems later converted back into mosques that are still there today, all on the same site. On Moriah the ramparts are all around, and behind Moriah the hilltops of Moab across the Jordan Valley swim in the far distance on pillows of pellucid air. We are at the meeting point of three climatic zones here, the Mediterranean, the central Asian steppe, and the desert, each with its own fauna and flora. As one pauses within sight of the city, stunned, on the edge of the fertile land, facing the stony wilderness and the rising sun, there seems to be no place like Jerusalem on the entire earth. From the air the view is even more breathtaking than from the ground.

It is an impression that no amount of familiarity can blunt. The city hangs on the watershed between the farmed land and the desert, which runs up almost to its gates. The bare, blue-gray hills open to a sudden view of swelling domes and towering minarets. A long line of wall, massive and imposing on its first-century base of colossal stones, is surmounted by a golden dome, superbly built, lustrous with Persian tiles against the translucent sky, a magnificent peacock rising from an immense stone platform. The sky above burns like a heated opal through the air; the walled-in mass of battlements within battlements and domes and churchtowers and minarets resembles nothing less than a ship sailing above the deep ravine into the tawny stone of the nearby wilderness. The very name Zion denotes its being "waterless," "parched," from the Hebrew *ziya*. And beyond the old city, with its ramparts and towers and elaborate gates that fewer than one hundred years ago still opened directly onto the desert mountainside, is the new modern city of close to half a million inhabitants.

Few capitals lie so high, or are so wonderful to look at and at the same time so terrifying. Jerusalem leans against the lunar background of the desert, a dazzling expanse, similar to a vast sea. It is the very epicenter of a turbulent country, where faith and superstition have alternated frequently and belief has too often been distorted into zealous fury and sectarian prejudice and persecution. The contradictions seem embedded in the landscape on both sides of the watershed that runs through the center of Jerusalem—in the sharp contrast between the greenery and forest west of the watershed and the desert east of it toward the Dead Sea. In Hebrew the very name *Yerushalaim* implies a duality, a pair of things, a parity between the desert and the sown, the heavenly and the earthly, between peace and war, goodliness and sin. Here fiction has too often found sites for miracles, and fables have usurped the place of history. Here among the stones the Jews first began to live morally—as the Japanese did literally—in a house of paper, the Bible. Recorded history goes back here for at least three thousand years; archeological remains date back almost that long; and the traveler in Jerusalem often finds himself in the position of the fabled hero who tied his horse to a wayside cross in the snow only to later find it dangling from the spire of what had been a buried church. In Jerusalem, even the nonbeliever must confront and come to terms with the phenomenon of faith and its concomitant sacredness. It is not necessary to believe the myths to be facts: the very existence of a myth is a great fact itself. Here, according to the Bible, David "danced before the Lord with all his might" and carried into the city, behind a curtain, the god whose image nobody had ever seen and most outsiders mocked. Here was waged the first long battle between the graven, sensual gods of the plain and the invisible god of the mountain. It is an austere, forbidding site, chosen with an unerring eye to house the temple of the cruel deity of an eye for an eye and a tooth for a tooth. The hills are massed around it, their names at once cherished and dreadful: Hill of Evil Counsel, Hill of Offense, Mount Zion, and Mount Olivet.

The singular beauty of Jerusalem seems to derive from a rare combination of luminosity and bareness. Everything is open to the sky. Here Isaiah cried in the wilderness. Here Jesus wept and bore the crown of thorns and was crucified with thieves. Here, according to the Koran, Mohammed came on his Night Journey and rode to heaven astride the winged white steed. Here the Crusaders marched, contrite but ankle-deep in blood, up the hill of Calvary—a weird union of the vilest and most tender passions, judged by some as "natural" and by others as "absurd and incredible." Here, for almost two thousand years, the Jews have prayed—from at least the twelfth century, three times daily at the present Western (or Wailing) Wall that they might "Return in mercy to your city Jerusalem and dwell in it as you have promised, rebuild it soon in our own days."

Jerusalem might have remained a small hill town. But she became sacred to three great religions, a city of strife, which continues to our own days: among warring Palestinians and Israelis; rival sects of Christians and of Jews; and the observant and the secular. Few major cities on earth have been so often or so cruelly besieged or so torn apart by internal dissent. Jerusalem has seen at least twenty major sieges and assaults—three of which involved the total destruction of its walls and buildings and a complete break in continuity, its natives sold into slavery or banished for ever—and at least twenty other military occupations that caused the partial destruction and dismantlement of the main edifices. Jerusalem has seen eight abrupt passages from one dominant religion to another. Nevertheless, it is a city of dramatic, almost enforced continuity. Like Cairo and Babylon, it is more than five thousand years old. But unlike in Cairo or Babylon, the principal language spoken today in Jerusalem is essentially the same as that spoken three thousand years ago by David to his men as they prepared to storm a small citadel known as Ir HaJebusi on the steep shelf below the present Temple Mount.

Standing there today at the precipice above the ravine, where, it is said, the Last Judgment will take place, one looks down—or up—on history itself. The Jerusalem name first crops up on a sherd of the third millennium B.C., at Ebla (an excavation in present-day Syria); it reoccurs more than a millennium later on a number of Egyptian clay tablets sent from Jerusalem by Abd Khiba, the city's ruler, to his Egyptian overlord. Abd Khiba invokes no deity; he only protests his undying loyalty to Pharaoh and his perpetual loneliness and fear in these mountains, surrounded by so many enemies. What a strange, prescient prelude to the city's future history! The Bible refers to Salem, the city of *El Elyon*, ("Most High God" and possibly a prototype of Yahweh); the Assyrians speak of Urusalimo, the "habitation of peace," and of the "god Salem," who seems to have been the titular deity here in the days of Abraham. Abraham called the place *Yira* ("vision"?; "dread"?). The Greeks identified it with Homer's Solymi. The Romans, after the destruction of A.D. 120, renamed it Aelia Capitolina. The Jews made Jerusalem the high place of an invisible god, and thus, as Edmund Wilson has written, they gave it to the whole human race.

Today the new city spreads for miles over the hills. But only in the north does the new impose upon the old and touch upon the ancient walls. Otherwise, the old city stands visually apart within its walls. It is surrounded by parks and cemeteries and by the deep ravines of Kidron and of Hinnom. Until the middle of the last century there were few houses outside the gates. The country on three sides reached the town walls. As soon as one emerged from one of the six town gates, which were open only during daylight, one was in the open country. Its bleak, brooding beauty had changed little since biblical times. When Ernest Renan wrote his life of Jesus in 1861, he included this countryside among his authoritative sources as a "fifth" Gospel. (The first four were, or course, Matthew, Mark, Luke, and John.) No one, he wrote, could understand the Bible and the origins of Christianity unless he knew the country. Before he sat down to describe Jesus's entry into Jerusalem, Renan climbed among the debris in the heat and dust to reconstruct in his mind the scene where Jesus told the multitude that "there shall not be left here one stone upon the other." Renan mastered the locale and imbued his account with a new kind of factual authenticity. Archaeologists, geographers, and ethnologists have since added to the record and vastly expanded our understanding of ancient history and geography. Today it is even stranger to reflect, or to wonder as Edmund Wilson did, how from these bare hills and pale contours came the legends that inspired the blazing colors of the Renaissance and the Baroque—that teeming of flesh and gorgeous silks and velvet, the beautiful blond Madonnas, the blue-eyed shepherds, Bathsheba in her bath, Susanah and the Elders in the lush surroundings of near Arcadian bliss, or at least fertility. It is as curious to note that in the Bible itself, the concrete features of this countryside, its cities and villages, are barely recorded except in a most general and abstract sense. Compare its style with that of the almost contemporary *Iliad* and *Odyssey* of Homer, both of which are so rich in vivid descriptions of great accuracy and plasticity. The comparison brings out an important feature of the ancient Hebrew civilization. Homer gives a clear sense of place. He appeals to the eye as well as to the ear. But the Bible appeals to the ear, and its descriptions of places and people are ephemeral. We are told that Jerusalem, or Jacob's wife, Rachel, was beautiful but not why or how. We are not given anything to convey a sense of plan—no shapes, no color or perspective, no interiors, few exteriors, no texture. The Bible tells us nothing of the dramatic, three-dimensional character of Jerusalem, to a modern eye so reminiscent of Toledo in Goya's famous painting. The reason for this absence of visual detail seems clear. The Greeks were a people of the eye and the visual form. The ancient Hebrews were a people of the ear, or, as Martin Buber wrote, they were a people of the *Anruf.* God appeared to them as sound, not as vision. Hence the appeals "Hear O Israel." In an incomparable scene in the Bible (Exodus 20:18), God descended upon Mount Sinai in fire, "and all the people *saw* the *thunderings*" (the Hebrew original says they "saw the *sound*").

When God's angel calls to Abraham—or to some prophet—he is answered "*Hineni*" (behold, here I am), but we rarely know where he is. The Bible has its clear order of priorities. We are given a minute, detailed description of the Ark of the Covenant, but of Jerusalem we are told only that it is "builded as a city that is compact together" (Psalm 122). No story in the Bible is as vivid as David's, at once human and dramatic, and under the stress of great passions: David as a lover, David as a friend, David as a rebel outcast, David listening to the complaints of his soldiers against himself, David tenderly warmed by a young maiden through the cold and feebleness of old age. And yet we never get a visual sense of where all this drama and melodrama are taking place. The prophets too foresee, but do not see: Jeremiah only *hears* across the land the noise of many people at Anathot, one of the most extraordinary landscapes in the Holy Land, a few miles north of Jerusalem overlooking the Dead Sea. Nor are the Gospels any different in this sense, although they were apparently originally written in Greek. Unlike the works of Homer, or any number of later Greek authors might have, they tell us nothing about the shape, or look, or feel of things on the Mount of Olives as Jesus sat there among his disciples, crying "O Jerusalem, Jerusalem, thou that killest the prophets" (Matthew 23:37).

Standing on Mount Olivet today, among the tourists, the vendors of souvenirs and cold drinks, and the camels for hire to mount and be photographed on, you look out on the right to the new campus of the Hebrew University on Mount Scopus. Scopus stands 2,736 feet above sea level. Up there it can be freezing cold in the winter, and the university, with its ultramodern facilities and computers linked by satellite with similar research facilities all over the globe, might be buried under snow.

Then you look down to your left. The road runs down the mountain to Jericho (820 feet below sea level), the lowest and the oldest town on earth, some twenty minutes away. In Jericho it is eternal summer among the palms and the flowering mangoes and flame trees. Tents of the Bedouin, recently come across the river Jordan from the wild Ghor like the Hebrew tribes in the Middle Bronze Age, are pitched alongside an ancient canal. In this country, in one short afternoon, you may have your pick of the climate and the century of your choice.

The road to Jericho passes through the bare, roughly hewn wilderness. The heat soars out of the Jordan Valley far below and singes the skin. Above the vast, desolate expanse of parched, dead soil, the sky rises in a blinding glare. Across the river valley, on the other side, glows the mountain wall of Moab. From Moab, Moses saw the Promised Land but could not enter. Judging from what you see today, it cannot have been a rose garden nor a land of milk and honey. At noon in this weird wasteland between Jerusalem and Jericho, the glare hangs over, and on the burnt-out ground are only blacks and whites—as in the mind of a fanatic, no shadows or muted colors in between. The sheer drop from the top of the mountain to the Dead Sea—the lowest spot on earth—is more than three thousand feet.

There are views here that few countries can match for sheer drama and contrast: the first view of the Dead Sea below, white with vast encrustations of salt, like packed ice in the arctic; the view up from Jericho toward the Jebel Quarantal, with its monastery and little chapels carved into the sharp, steep mountainside on the site traditionally identified as the Mount of Temptation; the mountains of Moab in the afternoon, pink, yellow, and bare. The monastery of St. George clings to the cliff of the Wadi Kelt, and nearby is Mar Saba, both occupied by hermits and monks continuously from the fourth century, when over a hundred such monasteries existed in the area. Only a few miles from Mar Saba are the remains of Qumran—the community center of the Essenes where the Dead Sea scrolls were found—the very first of these great cavernous retreats for men and women who did not flee the world but, believing that they could live here more fully, fervently filled the caves with messianic hopes and speculations. Many were leading scholars and prominent in the affairs of their time. And, south of Qumran, about halfway along the Dead Sea shore, stands the great rock of Masada; like Jerusalem it resembles a magnificent ship sailing on the edge of time into the surrounding wilderness. Masada was the scene of one of the most dramatic events in ancient history, the mass suicide of the Jewish zealots, men, women, and children who had withdrawn here after the fall of Jerusalem to make a last, hopeless stand against the Romans. Masada is probably the most spectacular site of them all.

Jericho, the green oasis at the northern end of the Dead Sea, is as lush and fertile from the air as it is on the ground. An elaborate grid of small, intersecting canals bears witness to its wealth and ample, but carefully regulated water reserves. It is the oldest town of which we know; here man built citadels for war and forged arrowheads of stone even before he domesticated certain animals and plants. Ancient Greeks and Romans spread Jericho's fame as a major producer of dates and balsam. In the Bible Jericho was "the city of palm trees," and of "Rahab the harlot," the city whose walls had come down flat at the sound of Joshua's trumpets. The extravagant claim in the Mishnah that in Jericho one could hear the Levites singing in the temple in Jerusalem emphasized the proximity of the two cities, even at the time when traffic was mostly on foot. Flying over it, you are back up the mountains in a few minutes. The mountain range north of Jerusalem seems forbidding and austere, with patches of light green on the dark brown earth and vistas down the deep valleys that run west from the watershed to the sea and east into the desert. Over Nablus, the ancient Shechem, you reach the famous point from which, on a clear day, the whole land, "from Dan to Beersheba," can be seen through a pair of medium-powered binoculars. The major physical features of the country are clearly visible—the four parallel strips of plain-mountain-desert-plain—as well as most of the famous sites of its history. Toward the north, above the haze, lies the snow-capped summit of Mount Hermon, to the west the sea, to the south the massed mountains sweeping down almost to the Negev Desert, and to the east the great wide gulf of the Jordan Valley that runs from the Lake of Tiberias down to the Dead Sea. Directly below, in Nablus, are the twin mountains of Ebal and Gerizim, and between them the highway by which, says the Bible, the patriarch Abraham first entered Canaan from Ur of the Chaldees. On this highway the famous promise "Unto thy seed will I give this land" was first uttered. The highway is now a main thoroughfare in the Palestinian Arab city of Nablus. The houses of Nablus climb halfway up the hills of Ebal and Gerizim, but their summits remain bare.

Behind Ebal, in the high tableland, lie the remains of a great Roman forum of the Second and Third centuries. The magnificent columns stand on the ruins of Samaria, which, the Bible tells us, was the capital of the kingdom of Israel in the eighth and seventh centuries B.C., before its destruction by the Assyrians. The land is more open here than uphill, and this is, perhaps, the reason why we read of so many chariots in these parts, and rarely if ever in Jerusalem. This is King Ahab's countryside, and that of his wicked queen, Jezebel. The story in I Kings (22:38) of Ahab's gruesome funeral comes to mind: they "washed the chariot in the pool of Samaria; and the dogs licked up his blood."

The farther north you now fly the more pleasant the land becomes. Yizrael (Esdraelon) is the wide valley behind Samaria. Yizrael was the home of the tribe of Issachar; its early fertility is well drawn in the picturesque biblical metaphor:

> Issachar is a strong ass
> couching down between two burdens:
> And he saw that rest was good,
> and the land that it was pleasant (Genesis 49:14–15).

It has been said of Yizrael that for the highlander looking down on it from Samaria it must have seemed an unusually pleasant land with ample room in which to stretch and lie happy. Much of it was swamp or given to weeds when the first Jewish settlers came here early in this century. Nowadays it is full of prosperous kibbutzim. The kibbutzim work the fertile land and grow fish in the large ponds. From the air the ponds are huge mirrors at the foot of Mount Gilboa. On Gilboa, the Bible tells us, the wounded Saul fell on his sword and David cursed the hills in his dirge:

> Ye mountains of Gilboa,
> let there be no dew,
> neither let there be rain upon you,
> nor fields of offerings (2 Samuel 1:21).

Some of them are still bare. On others intensive afforestation has been accomplished in recent years. Gilboa stands like a wall south of the valley of Yizrael. Directly ahead is Mount Tabor, like a huge breast rising out of the plain. And what a plain it is, in the history of warfare as well as of religion! From the days of Thutmose III to those of Napoleon, who routed the Turks at the foot of Tabor shortly before himself being beaten outside of Acre. Tabor as a holy mountain has excited awe and wonder since the dawn of history (the name derives from the Hebrew *tabur,* meaning navel, center, or birthplace of the earth). For the Psalmist, Tabor bore witness to the glory of God; Christian tradition locates there the transfiguration of Christ: "And [he] was transfigured before them: and his face did shine as the sun, and his raiment was white as the light" (Matthew 17:2).

Behind Tabor lies Nazareth. Again, the farther north you look the greener the countryside appears. This is not because more rain falls in the Galilee, but because the sea breeze wafts in moisture and the dew is more abundant. There is no desert wind, as there is in Jerusalem, to infect the countryside with austerity. This is the rich farmland of Asher—

"Asher his bread shall be fat, and he shall yield royal dainties," as it says in Genesis (49:20). There is a profusion of brush, shrub, and forest, flowers, corn, and oil.

Turning west you look upon the battlefield of Megiddo (Armageddon) where so many empires and faiths contended and so many battles were fought that in Jerusalem "the great mourning in the valley of Megiddo" was proverbial. And in the east, the lovely Sea of Galilee (actually a lake) shimmers in the sun. The lake narrows at its southern end. It lies harp-shaped (hence its Hebrew name Kinneret, *kinor* meaning "harp") below the terraced hills of lower Galilee. The rabbis said, "God created seven seas but the Sea of Kinneret is his delight." The first-century historian Josephus Flavius was equally enthusiastic as he described the shores of the lake, where, he wrote, the soil was so fertile and the climate so well blended that all sorts of fragrant flowers and fruit trees grew in great profusion all year long. The trees today—there are a great many—are mostly of recent origin. Fifty years ago the cliffs surrounding the lake were still arid moor, strewn with huge boulders of lava and pumice stone. When the first Zionist pioneers arrived on the southern shore in 1909, there were no trees except, probably, one lonely palm, of which the poetess Rachel Bluwstein, one of the pioneers, wrote: "By the sea of Galilee, a stunted tattered palm."

Many trees now stand in thickets, and tall cypresses and carobs and oaks line the wide strip of park between the sea and the little white houses along the shore. It is a soft, dreamy landscape, strangely, almost mystically transfigured on a hazy day, a land of utopian dreams, a meeting point of the real and the imagined. In the tranquil atmosphere of the mountain lake, Jesus moved among simple fishermen and preached a gospel of love and of peace; it is difficult to imagine a more fitting setting. Here too, the first kibbutz was established in 1911, intended by its founders to be another Eden, a kingdom of saints in a new world purged of suffering and sin. Its founders lie buried today in a little graveyard by the lake, like a race of seafarers. Their descendants live in neat little houses shaded by huge trees. In the distance you see the modern resort town of Tiberias, and Tabha and Capernaum, where Christ pronounced the Beatitudes. The Jordan River enters the lake through a narrow gorge in the north and exits in the south, shaded by heavy eucalyptus trees. The thick undergrowth covers both banks all along its serpentine course. The Jordan amazes by its narrowness: it is a brook by European or American standards. It does not roll. It trickles. But in the distance the snow-capped summit of Mount Hermon rises majestically above the clouds.

The Holy Land. The Heavenly and the Earthly in a land of dreams, some gorgeous, others perfectly wild. In this book, in Richard Nowitz's wonderful sequence of aerial photographs, we have tried to show a little of both.

OPPOSITE: Old stone quarries in the coastal plain north of Lod, southeast of Tel Aviv.

OVERLEAF: The valley of Ayalon, in the Judean foothills between the coastal plain and the Judean Hills; according to the Bible, Joshua made the moon stand still here and the sun at Gibeon.

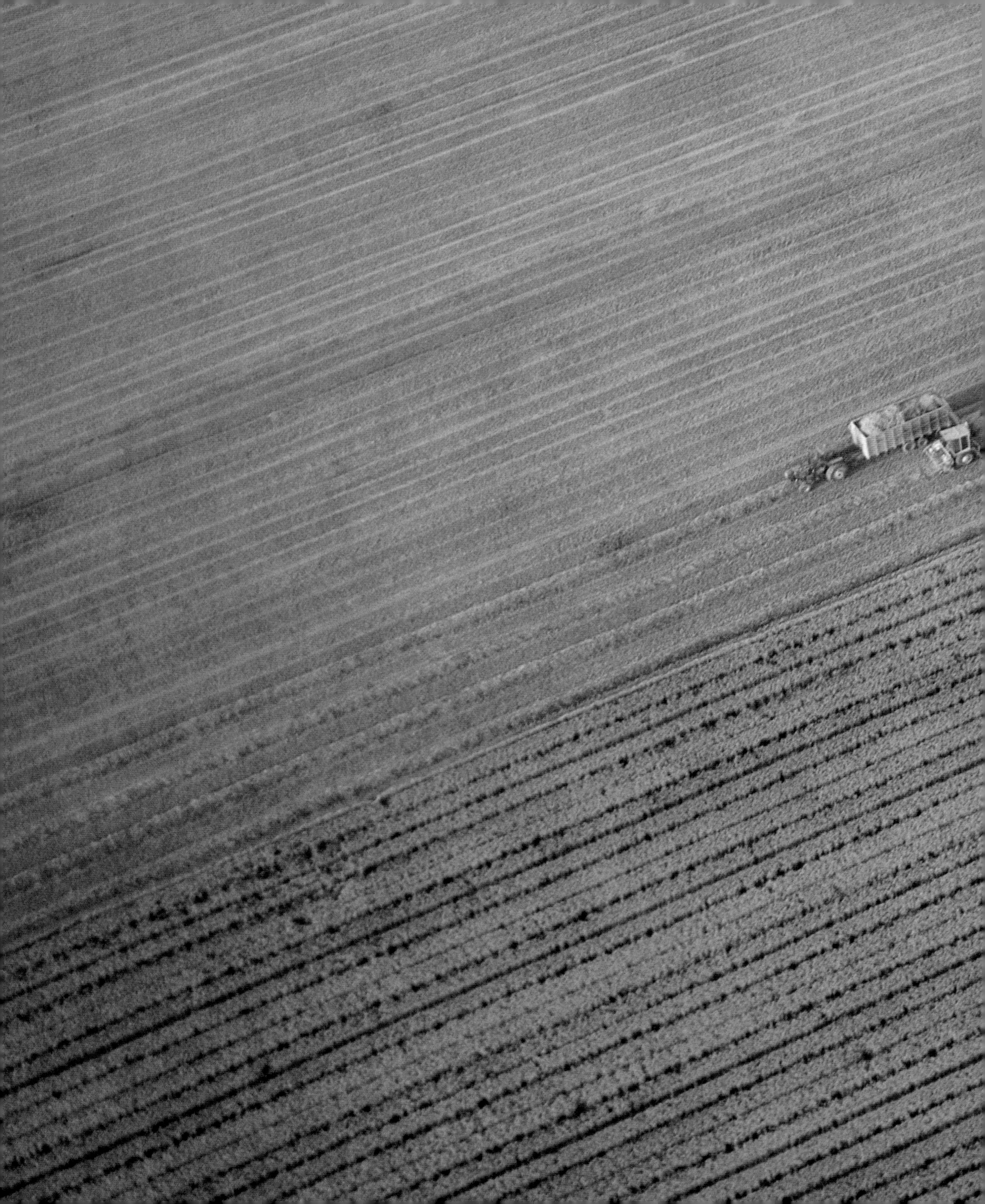

ABOVE: Tel Aviv, the economic and social center of Israel and the first all-Jewish city in modern Israel, was founded in 1908 as a garden suburb of old Jaffa. Literally "Hill of Spring," it may well be the only major city in the world today named after a book—Theodor Herzl's utopian novel of 1903, *Altneuland*, translated into Hebrew as *Tel Aviv* ("Then I came to them of the captivity at Tel-abib"; Ezekiel 3:15).

OPPOSITE: Old Jaffa on the Mediterranean shore. The site is one of the oldest continuously inhabited places in the world. It is mentioned in the list of port cities conquered by Thutmose III in the sixteenth century. To the "haven of Joppa" cedars of Lebanon were sent in floats for the building of successive temples in Jerusalem. Until the 1920s, when the port of Haifa was dug, Jaffa was the main seaport and trading center of the Holy Land and the pilgrims' gate to Jerusalem. Ships moored at some distance from the shore, and passengers were ferried in through a series of protruding rocks to which, according to Greek myth, Andromeda had been chained by the dragon. The first Zionist pioneers came ashore here in 1882. Today Jaffa is a part of the metropolitan area of Tel Aviv. The little port serves only fishing and pleasure boats.

OVERLEAF: One of the two Roman aqueducts at Caesarea built in the time of Herod.

ABOVE: Prehistoric caves near Zichron Yaakov, a wine-making village on the western slope of Mount Carmel.

OPPOSITE: Caesarea, on the Mediterranean coast about halfway between Haifa and Jaffa, was the capital city under Roman and Byzantine rule and later a Crusader fortress. It was renowned in the ancient world for the splendor of its buildings and the spectacles held in its circus and theater, seen here. Inside the theater was found a Latin inscription commemorating Pontius Pilate, "who made and dedicated this Tibereum to the Divine Augustus."

OVERLEAF: An uninviting coast: there is barely a break in the long line where land and sea meet on the Mediterranean south of Tel Aviv. The maritime plain is a narrow strip of greens, browns, and yellows.

ABOVE: Rishon le-Zion ("First to Zion," as in Isaiah 41:27, who "will give to Jerusalem . . . good tidings") was the first modern Jewish colony, founded in 1882 by Zionist settlers escaping anti-Semitic riots in czarist Russia. In the 1930s it was known for its vineyards and citrus groves, most of which have since been uprooted to make room for the modern city that Rishon le-Zion is today.

OPPOSITE: The Mediterranean coast south of Nathania, a large resort city named after the American philanthropist Nathan Straus. There are no offshore islands nor any deep estuaries along this coast.

OVERLEAF: Bahai sanctuary at Haifa, Israel's third largest city, its main port, and a large industrial and cultural center at Mount Carmel.

Acre—the Crusaders' St. Jean d'Acre—is still visually a medieval city. The separate quarters built by the city-states of Pisa, Venice, Amalfi, and Genoa for their merchants and sailors are well preserved to this day. The Great Mosque *(left)* at the entrance of the old city was built in 1781 by the Turks, who eighteen years later, aided by a British fleet at anchor in the harbor, successfully defended Acre against Napoleon and his forces.

OVERLEAF: Athlit, or Château Pelerin, which the Crusaders built in 1218 for the protection of the Christian pilgrims. It projects into the sea between two shallow bays. Excavations have shown that the site was inhabited from remote times, certainly by the Phoenicians in the tenth century B.C.

ABOVE: Nabi Musa, venerated by Muslims as the tomb of Moses, is located in the Judean Desert, just before the descent into the Jordan Valley.

OPPOSITE: In the summer of 1947 a Bedouin shepherd boy pursued a runaway goat along the cliffs of Qumran that rim the northwest coast of the Dead Sea and came upon an unknown cave. He threw a stone into the cave and heard the sound of breaking clay. It was thus that one of the most important archaeological finds of the century came to light—the Dead Sea Scrolls. The cave is in the cliffs behind the excavated ruins, the remains of a community center built by the Essenes, the sect that produced the scrolls. Most of the scrolls themselves are now located in the Israel Museum in Jerusalem; some are at the Shrine of the Book.

OVERLEAF: The wilderness of the Judean Hills between Jerusalem and the Dead Sea.

ABOVE: Monastery of Der Nejlu, now abandoned, on the salt soil of the northern shore of the Dead Sea.

OPPOSITE: Mar Saba, named after St. Sabas (439–532), who built the first monastery in this wild gorge east of Bethlehem in the Judean Desert in 482. It is a remarkable fact that even though by the fifth century Christianity was well established as the official religion of a powerful empire, and its adherents were no longer persecuted but offered security, still hundreds of thousands of Christians apparently left the comforts of home to withdraw to secluded desert spots such as this. The largest Judean Desert monastery for 1,500 years, today Mar Saba is one of the oldest occupied monasteries in the world, peopled by almost a dozen monks of the Greek Orthodox church.

OVERLEAF: Sheep corral in the Judean Desert. Shepherding is one of the few occupations feasible in this dry, inhospitable area.

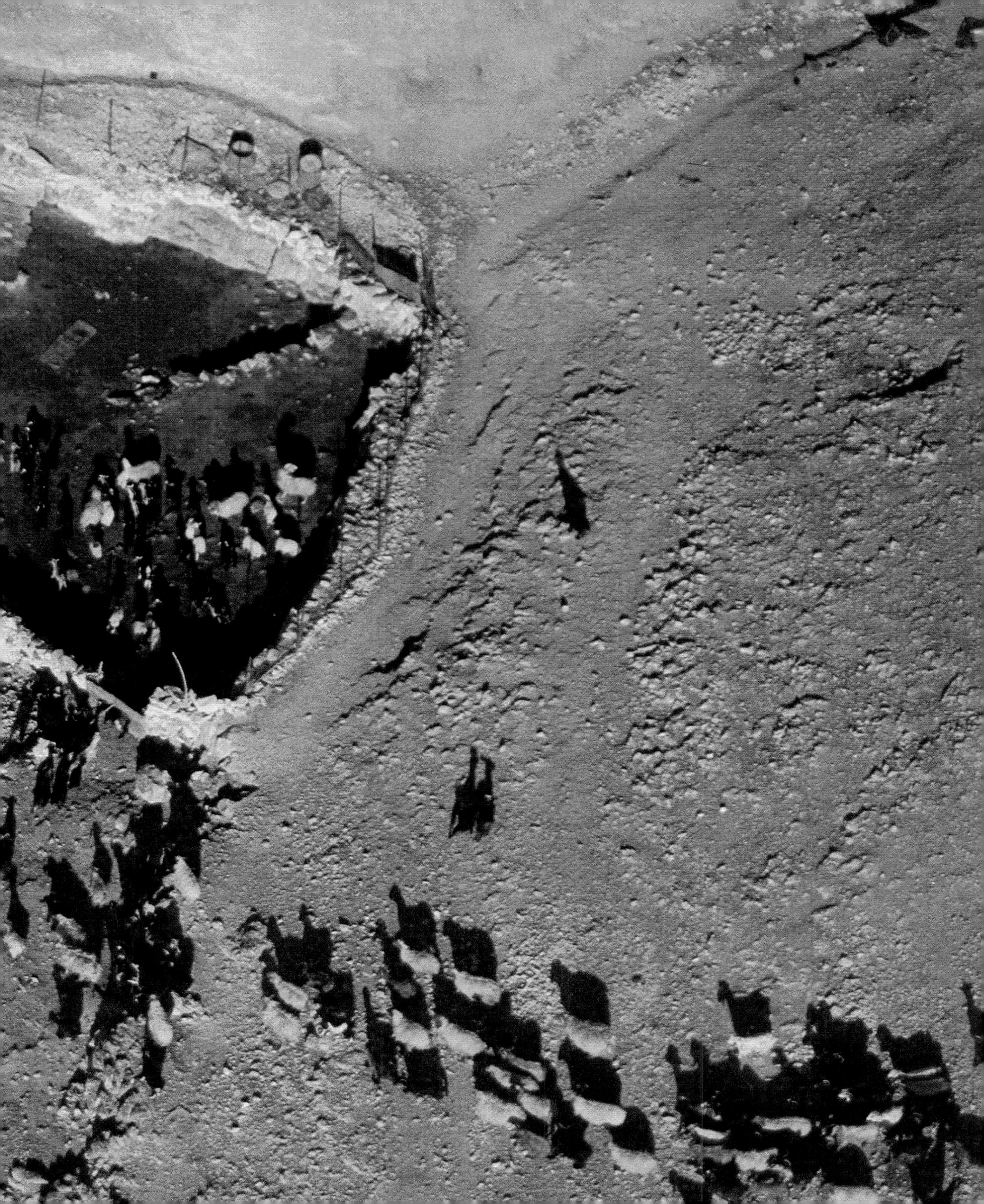

ABOVE: Hebron, 18 miles south of Jerusalem, one of the oldest continuously inhabited cities in the world, is venerated by Jews, Christians, and Moslems as the burial place of the patriarchs Abraham, Isaac, and Jacob and their spouses. The cave of Machpelah is now a mosque (Haram el Khalil) in which, since 1967, Jewish prayer services also take place. The cave is enclosed within a colossal Herodian wall built in superbly cut mammoth stones, similar to the Western Wall in Jerusalem.

LEFT: Herodion, Herod the Great's fortress-palace four miles southeast of Bethlehem on the way to Masada and almost 2,500 feet above sea level, is reminiscent of Roman imperial tombs. Herod commanded to be buried here together with a vast fortune in gold and silver, but so far extensive excavations have found no trace of either his tomb or any treasure.

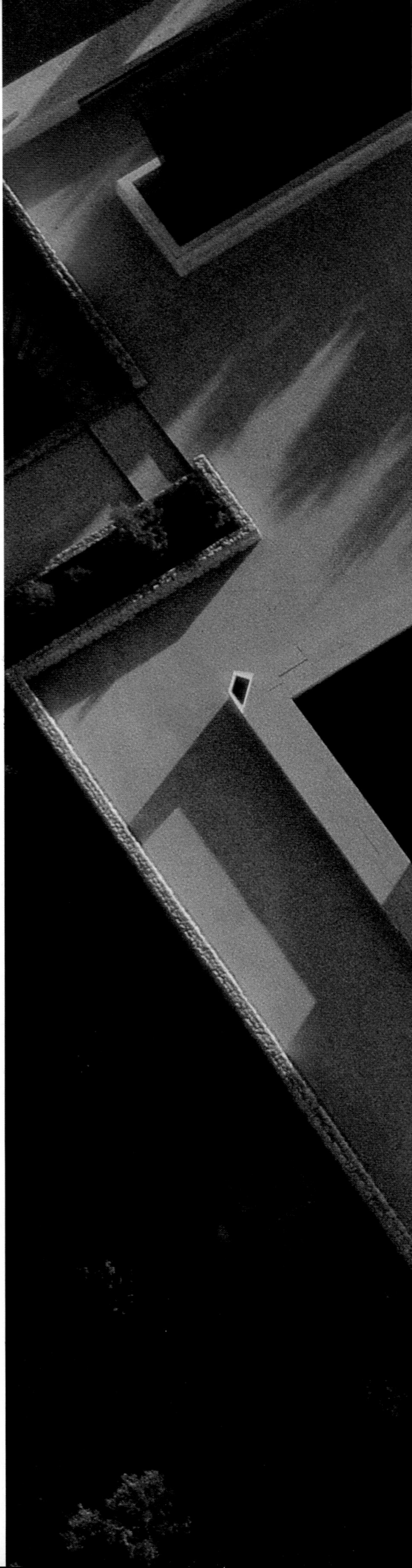

RIGHT: The Shrine of the Book within the Israel Museum complex in Jerusalem houses the best of the Dead Sea Scrolls and other first and second century manuscripts found in the caves of Qumran in the Judean Desert. Its pointed round roof is intended to represent the cover of one of the clay jars in which the Dead Sea Scrolls were found.

OVERLEAF: The western part of Jerusalem, with the Shrine of the Book, and the Knesseth, Israel's parliament, in the background. In the foreground is the Israel Museum sculpture garden.

Ain Kerem, the biblical Beth Kerem, in the hills southwest of Jerusalem. Excavations have revealed traces of an inhabited center during the Bronze Age, but Ain Kerem is famous mainly as the traditional birthplace of St. John the Baptist. Its name (meaning Spring or House of the Vineyard) denotes the site's role as a wine-producing area in biblical times. "O ye children of Benjamin, gather yourselves to flee out of the midst of Jerusalem," said Jeremiah (6:1), "and blow the trumpet in Tekoa, and set up a sign of fire at Beth-haccerem." The New Testament does not mention Beth Kerem by name, only reports that Mary had gone in haste into the hill country outside Jerusalem to salute Elizabeth (Luke 1:39).

ABOVE: The twelve cupolas of the Roman Catholic Church of All Nations, at the foot of Mount Olivet, refer to the twelve nations which contributed funds to its construction. At left is the traditional site of the Garden of Gethsemane. A few ancient olive trees still stand there and bear fruit. The garden must have been on or very close to the direct route that in the first century led from the Temple Mount, across the valley, to the summit of Olivet. According to tradition many events related to the life of Jesus took place at this area: hence the many holy sites located here.

OPPOSITE: On the slope of Olivet is the Russian Church of St. Mary Magdalene, built in 1888 by Czar Alexander III in memory of his mother, with its seven characteristic onion-shaped turrets. A flight of ancient steps cut in the rock leads from here to the summit of Olivet.

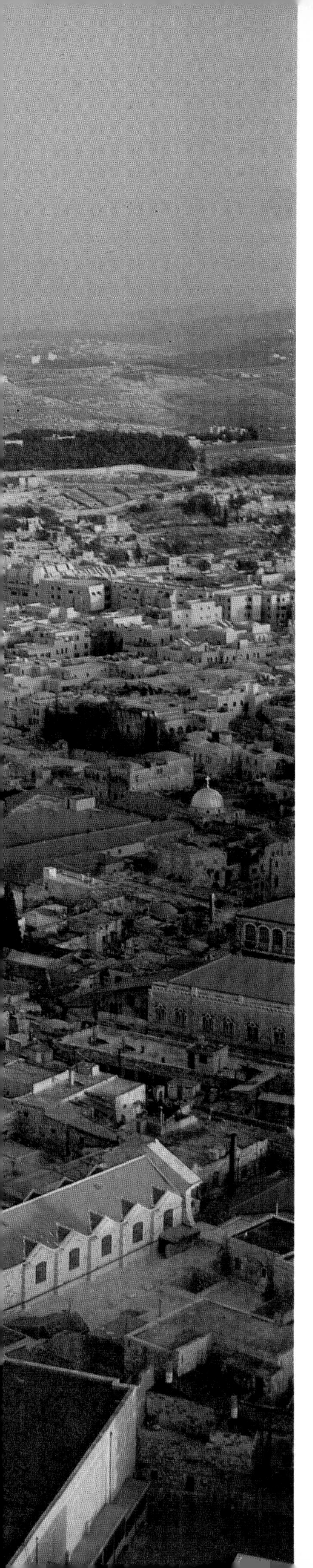

ABOVE: The Basilica of the Holy Sepulchre—the most venerated sanctuary in all Christendom—was built on the site identified since the fourth century with the passion and sepulchre of Christ on Calvary. Today it takes a good deal of imagination to envisage the splendor of the original basilica Constantine the Great built here on the site of a pagan temple in A.D. 325–35; or of that built by the Crusaders, said to have been one of the greatest structures of the twelfth century, a worthwhile companion, it seemed, to the contemporary cathedrals of Chartres and Vézelay. Its outlines can still be determined by the great rectangle formed by the shopfronts and bazaars in the top righthand corner of the picture. In Crusader times the entire rectangle still formed part of the basilica. The present church, a jumble of buildings connected by narrow corridors and chapels belonging to six rival sects, is squeezed in between two mosques and several bazaars. Few discerning visitors or pilgrims from the west have had much good to say about the basilica's present circumstances. It was not only the discovery, which to some had obviously come as a shock, that Christianity here was above all an *Eastern* religion, and that as an *Eastern* religion it had been kept alive during the so-called Dark Ages, but the basilica's aesthetics as well have often been criticized. In this latter aspect, things have changed for the better in recent years: plans for a common restoration of the dilapidated site are finally being implemented by the three main communities—the Latins, the Greeks, and the Armenians.

OPPOSITE: Jerusalem: the city hangs on the watershed between the sown and the desert. It faces the wilderness and the rising sun: a stupendous impression, which no amount of familiarity can blunt. In the east, behind the rooftops and towers, the pink and yellow mountains of Moab, luminous and bare, beckon in the distance. Note the proximity of the main holy sites of three religions: the large dome in the center is the Basilica of the Holy Sepulchre; immediately behind it is the Western Wall; to the left of the Western Wall, the Dome of the Rock on the Temple Mount.

BELOW: The golden dome of the seventh-century Dome of the Rock, designated by Moslem tradition as the spot from which Muhammad ascended to heaven on his night journey, is perhaps the most significant entity in all Jerusalem as well as one of the earliest and best examples of Moslem architecture in the world. Here a Jewish temple stood until A.D. 70, and later, a temple of Jupiter. Under the Crusaders the Dome of the Rock served as a Christian church.

ABOVE: The Jaffa Gate, one of eight gates in the wall of the old city of Jerusalem, stands at the road that leads to Jaffa. To the right, within the so-called Citadel of David, are the remains of three Herodian towers that Titus, when he razed Jerusalem in A.D. 70, left standing as monuments to the valor of his troops. The citadel had in all probability been the palace of Herod the Great: "Adjoining and on the inner side of the towers," wrote Joseph Flavius, the first-century Jewish historian, "was the king's palace, baffling all description" (*Jewish War*, 5:173). Later on, Pontius Pilate, the Roman procurator, has his residence here; here also the trial of Jesus might have taken place. In the background can be seen the Church of the Holy Sepulchre and the Dome of the Rock; behind them, across the valley of Kidron, is Mount Olivet.

LEFT: Temple Mount, or Moriah, where according to legend Abraham made ready to sacrifice Isaac and where Herod built the First and Second Jewish Temples, has been a national and religious focal point of the Jewish people for many generations. At top left is the Dome of the Rock; at lower right is the Western Wall, where for centuries Jews have come to pray and lament the destruction of the temple. The Western Wall originally formed part of the retaining wall built by Herod the Great in 20 B.C. to support the vast platform, still existing today, on which the temple stood. Prior to 1967 the old city houses came to within four meters of the Western Wall; they have since been razed to make place for the present plaza on which tens of thousands of people gather for prayers on the high Jewish holidays.

OVERLEAF: Suleiman the Magnificent, the Ottoman sultan, built the present ramparts in 1540 on the remnants of older Jewish, Roman, Arab, and Crusader walls. Of the six gates he built, all apparently designed by the same hand, the Damascus Gate is the most elaborate and perhaps the finest piece of Ottoman architecture in Jerusalem, as well as the largest of the entrances to the old city. Under the modern bridge leading into Jerusalem appear the excavated ruins of a beautiful, older Roman gate. Behind it, within the city wall, a huge column honoring the Roman emperor Hadrian must have stood (it is clearly marked on a sixth-century mosaic map). In Arabic the gate is still called *Bab el Amud* (Gate of the Column).

Jerusalem, it has often been said, is more thickly populated with the dead than with the living. "Men from all parts of the world come hither to die," Abu Muin Nasir, an Arab writer, wrote in 1047. The city is ringed by a huge necropolis. Its oldest part is in the east, along the valleys of Kedron and Yehoshafath, where according to legend the Last Judgment will take place, and on the slopes of Olivet.

ABOVE, LEFT AND RIGHT: Christian cemeteries behind the Church of the Ascension on the Mount of Olives.

OPPOSITE, ABOVE: For the ancient Hebrews, Olivet was a place of burial as well as of mourning: "And David went up by the ascent of mount Olivet, and wept as he went up, and had his head covered, and he went barefoot: and all the people that was with him covered every man his head, and they went up, weeping as they went up" (2 Samuel 15:30).

OPPOSITE, BELOW: Military cemetery on Mount Herzl, west of Jerusalem, a bitter reminder of the five wars Israel has fought since its foundation in 1948, and of the many bloody skirmishes in between.

ABOVE: The buttressed walls of the Greek Orthodox Monastery of the Cross rise in the valley bearing the same name, derived from the legend that the tree from which the cross on which Jesus was crucified was made had grown here. The area still abounds in ancient olive trees, which today form part of a large, public park.

OPPOSITE: The Romanesque church of St. Anne, the site, according to Christian tradition, of Mary's birth, is, in its simple strength, a perfect example of twelfth-century Crusader architecture. Next to it on the left are the excavated ruins of the twin pools of Bethesda.

ABOVE: Yemin Moshe, residential quarter, now considered to be an artists' quarter, was one of the first Jewish settlements outside the old city's walls when it was founded in the nineteenth century.

OPPOSITE: Mount Zion on the western hill projecting out beyond the southern wall of the old city. Before the destruction of Jerusalem in A.D. 70 the walls ran farther west and the hill was still enclosed within them. "Zion . . . shall be plowed as a field," it is said in Micah (3:12), "and Jerusalem shall become heaps." The great German Church of the Dormition (*center*), where Mary fell into eternal sleep, was built at the beginning of this century (1910).

ABOVE: Anathot, the Arab village in the Judean Hills just northeast of Jerusalem, believed to be the village where the prophet Jeremiah grew up, overlooks the Judean Desert. Behind the village the land falls away in a maze of broken rocks. The vision of that wilderness, blazing in the heat, may have been in Jeremiah's mind when he said: "A dry wind of the high places in the wilderness . . . not to fan, nor to cleanse" (4:11).

OPPOSITE: The campus of Hebrew University, opened in 1925, on Mount Scopus on the northeast side of Jerusalem.

ABOVE: Bethlehem, about four and one-half miles south of Jerusalem. In the center can be seen the Crusader Church of the Nativity, built over the remains of an earlier Byzantine basilica. "But thou, Bethlehem Ephratah, though thou be little among the thousands of Judah, yet out of thee shall he come forth unto me that is to be ruler in Israel" (Micah 5:2). According to the Old Testament, David, the second Jewish king, was born here. The emperor Constantine built the first basilica over the cave identified two centuries earlier by Justinus Martyr as the birthplace of Jesus. Constantine's mother, Helene, inaugurated the basilica in 339; until shortly before that the cave had been a sanctuary dedicated to the worship of Jupiter and Adonis. There are still today many houses in Bethlehem that are built over or in front of caves.

OPPOSITE: Shepherds Field, outside Bethlehem, identified with the place where Jacob pitched his tents after the death of Rachel and where the angel came upon the shepherds to announce the birth of Christ.

OVERLEAF: "Solomon's Pools," a complex of three large (the lowest is 580 feet long and 50 feet deep) pools that store spring water and catch rain water, south of Bethlehem. For centuries they have formed part of the extensive water supply system for Jerusalem. Elements of the system—aqueducts, reservoirs, and underground pipes—date back to the first century B.C., perhaps even earlier. Today the water from the pools is used only by inhabitants of the immediate vicinity.

ABOVE: Hula Valley, with Mount Hermon snow-covered in the distance. Now one of the most fertile parts of Galilee, Hula was a malaria-infested swamp until the early 1950s, when it was drained.

OPPOSITE: On the Via Maris ("Way of the Sea"), the principal caravan route between north and south and commanding a well-watered pass, Hatzor was a fortress city that made use of its strategic position between weaker neighbors to become "the head of all those kingdoms" (Joshua 11:10). In its heyday, between the seventeenth and eighteenth centuries B.C., the city occupied an area of almost two hundred acres. Archaeological evidence shows that the city was burned down in the second half of the thirteenth century; this has been tied to the account in Joshua 11:13 of the burning of Hatzor by the Israelites under Joshua. Hatzor reappears later in the Bible as a cavalry city built by Solomon.

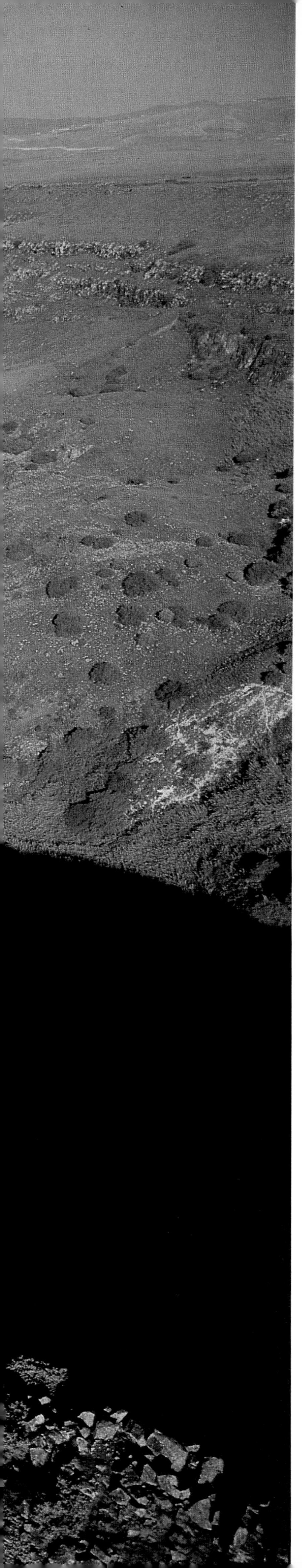

"And the Romans captured all the fortresses (of Galilee) . . . Gamala also which is a city on the other side of the lake . . . revolted against them (relying) on the difficulty of the place which was situated . . . upon a rough ridge of a high mountain, with a kind of neck in the middle . . . like a camel in figure, from whence it is so named" (Josephus Flavius, *Wars of the Jews*, 5:1).

Gamala (*left*) was a natural fortress on the Golan Heights above the Sea of Galilee. The saga of its siege and ultimate battle has been compared to that of Masada. After a long siege the Romans, in A.D. 67, finally scaled its ramparts, and the last of the fighting garrison withdrew to the citadel in the upper part. When they too were surrounded and "despaired of escaping," Josephus reports, they "flung their children and their wives, and themselves also, down the precipices. . . . The Romans slew four thousand, whereas the number that had thrown themselves down was found to be five thousand: nor did anyone escape except two women."

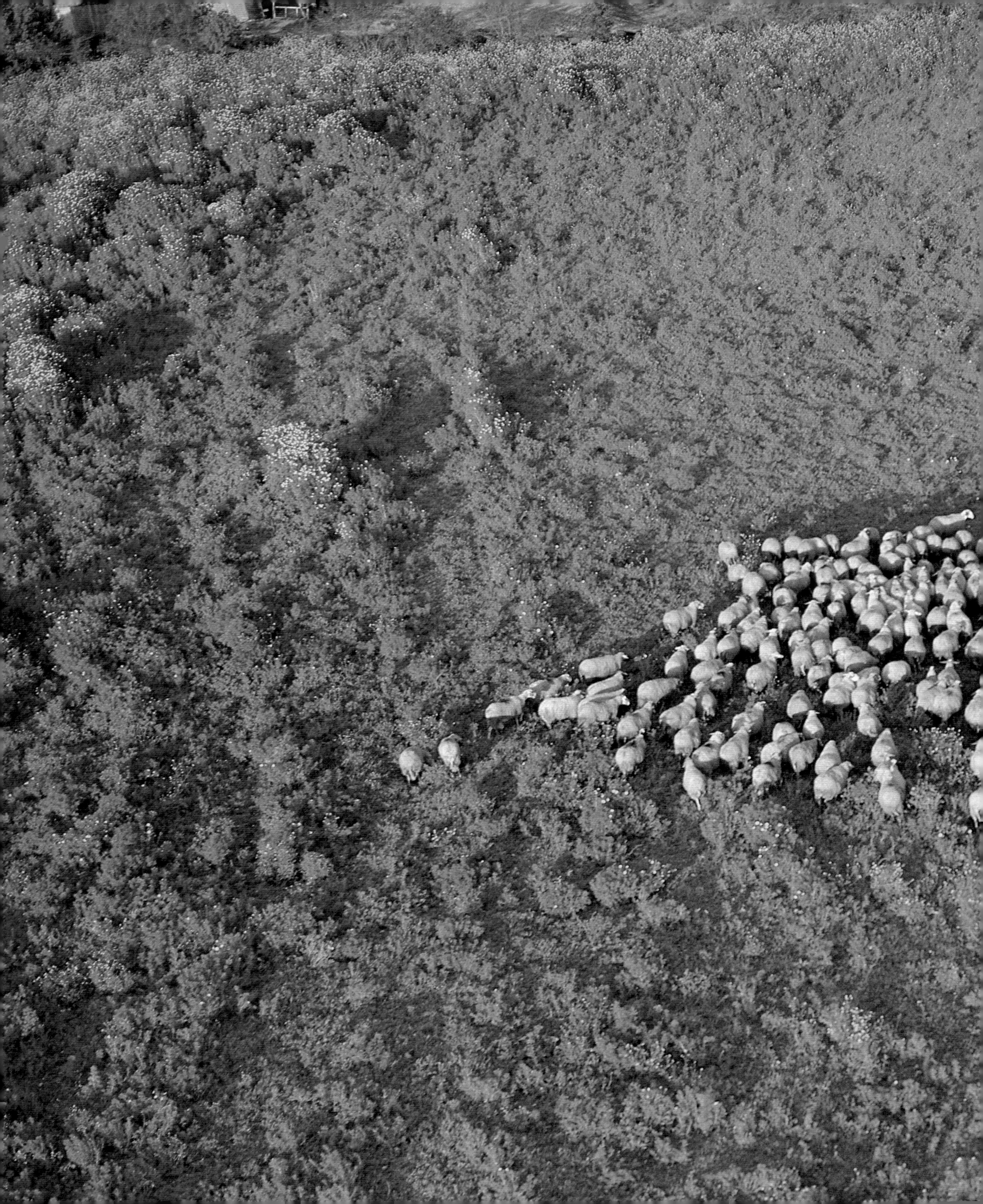

ABOVE AND OPPOSITE: Fields and fishponds, like huge reflecting mirrors, at the foot of the Gilboa mountain range. Some of the hilltops are still as dry and bare as they were in David's lament for Saul and Jonathan: "Ye mountains of Gilboa, let there be no dew, neither let there be rain, upon you, nor fields of offerings: for there the shield of the mighty is vilely cast away, the shield of Saul, as though he had not been anointed with oil" (2 Samuel 1:21).

OVERLEAF: Valley of Yizrael (Esdraelon) near Harod, the well where Gideon stood up to the Midianites (Judges 7:1). There are rich kibbutz lands around it today, and the well area with its natural pool is part of a national park.

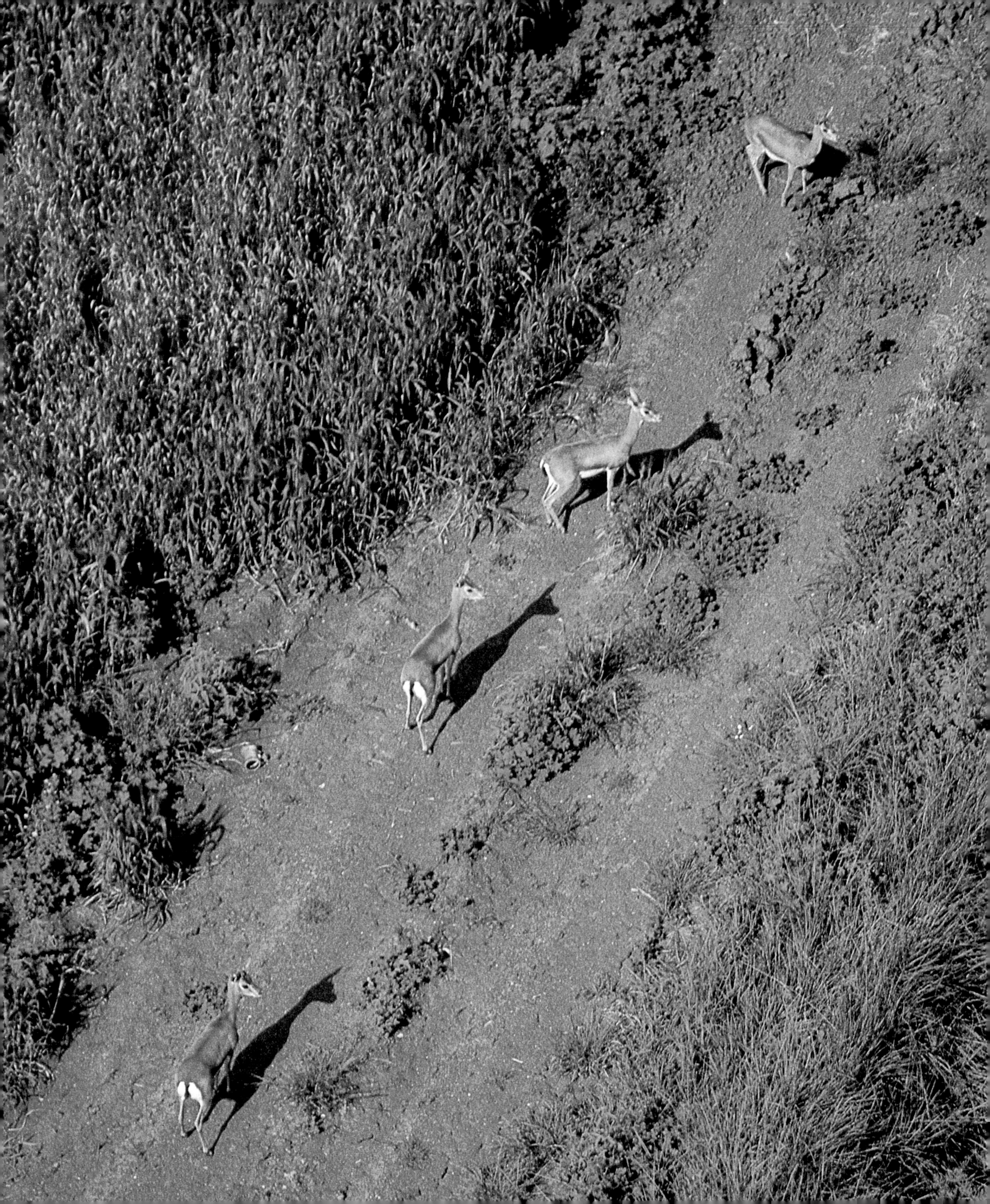

ABOVE: The Roman theater at Beth Shean, perhaps the best preserved in the country, testifies to the importance of that city in the first century. The Romans merely continued what had been begun thousands of years before. The natural advantages of the site, on the main west–east highway connecting Egypt and the sea with Mesopotamia, help to explain its long history. Beth Shean has been continuously occupied for more than five thousand years. Its 260-foot-high *tel* (mound) contains eighteen superimposed cities. It was one of the major strongholds from which the Pharaohs, the Philistines, the Hebrews, the Romans, and the Byzantines successively controlled the country.

OVERLEAF: The *moshav* (cooperative settlement) of Nahalal, at the mouth of the valley Yizrael. It was founded in 1921 as part of a great social experiment that continues to this day. Its circular shape was meant to serve (and symbolically reflect) an experiment in rational farming and town planning. The jointly owned services (tractor stations, marketing and purchasing agencies, clinics, schools, etc.) are at the center and are surrounded by a wide circle of equidistant farmhouses and individually owned fields. The *moshav* was a compromise between the collectivist kibbutz and the free enterprise village. It is today the most common form of farming in Israel.

ABOVE: Carmiel, a new city in Galilee founded in 1964 and settled mostly by new immigrants.

RIGHT: The excavations at Megiddo (Armageddon), with the battlefield in the background, reveal one of the great theaters of history, where so much blood was shed in so many battles between so many rival faiths and empires that the name has come to denote destruction in an ultimate, apocalyptic battle. Its position in the plain at the head of an important mountain pass gave it control over the Via Maris, the main highway between Egypt and the north, northeast. Thutmose III carved a graphic record of the battle he fought here in 1468 B.C. on the wall of his temple at Karnak in upper Egypt. Solomon built a palace at Megiddo and stables for his cavalry horses; some of their ruins have been excavated.

ABOVE: Church above the Sea of Galilee on the site where Jesus pronounced the Beatitutes. One is tempted to seek a natural link between a religion of love and this soft, dreamy landscape, as between the harsh and cruel desert land east of Jerusalem and the notion of "an eye for an eye and a tooth for a tooth." Josephus said that the air at the shore of the lake was "so well tempered that it suits the most opposite varieties . . . by a happy rivalry each of the seasons wished to claim this region for her own."

OPPOSITE: Near the church pictured above, the remains of a synagogue have been unearthed at Capernaum.

ABOVE: "We travelled to the city of Nazareth, where many miracles take place," the sixth-century Pilgrim of Piacenza wrote. "In the synagogue at Nazareth there is kept a book in which the Lord wrote his ABC, and in this synagogue is the bench on which he sat with other children." Already a century earlier the church father Epiphanius had complained that in Nazareth no one could build churches because the Jews were still in the majority there, as they apparently were all over the Galilee. Today Nazareth is the largest Arab town in Israel. The cityscape is dominated by the massive basilica of the Annunciation (*bottom left*) on the site where, according to Antonius Placentinus (A.D. 570), a former synagogue had been converted to a church.

OPPOSITE: National water carrier, north of Nazareth. Water is pumped from the sea of Galilee in the north to the Negev in the south.

OVERLEAF: Safad in upper Galilee, one of the fortresses during the revolt against the Romans of A.D. 67–70 listed by Josephus Flavius. After the fall of Jerusalem, Safad became a substantial Jewish religious center, and in the late middle ages the principal settlement in Palestine of Jewish scholars expelled from Spain. The first printing press in Palestine (a Hebrew press) was set up in Safad in 1563.

Summit of Mount Tabor (*above*) with basilica on the site first identified in 216 by Origenes with the transfiguration of Christ (*opposite*). The mountain soars suddenly 1,929 feet above the surrounding plain, and, probably because of its graceful form and picturesque site, it has excited awe and wonder since time immemorial. It has been a sacred mountain at least since the first millennium B.C. Hosea upbraided the Jews for building altars on Tabor to pagan gods. The road winds in hairpin bends up its sides through the striking vegetation of evergreen oaks, lentisks, and carob trees, and from the summit there is a stupendous panorama.

ABOVE: The ancient synagogue at Tiberias, on the shore of the Sea of Galilee. Founded by Herod Antipas (4 B.C.–A.D. 39), the son of Herod the Great, and named after his patron, the emperor Tiberius, the synagogue was an important center of Jewish learning until the fifth century, and again in the middle ages.

RIGHT: Kinereth, the first kibbutz, founded in 1911. The kibbutz was not a premeditated creation by convinced ideologues: the idea developed out of the practical needs of early settlers.

OVERLEAF: Cliffs of Arbel on the western shores of the Sea of Galilee.

ABOVE: Roman theater in Samaria, on the ruins of the eighth-century capital of the (northern) kingdom of Israel. Micah warned, "I shall make Samaria as an heap of the field" (1:6), but Jeremiah said, "Thou shalt yet plant vines upon the mountains of Samaria" (31:5).

OPPOSITE AND OVERLEAF: The Wadi Farah, a perennial stream, runs from the heights of Samaria through arid land down some 3,700 feet to the Jordan valley. Abraham is thought to have come up the Wadi Farah, after crossing the Jordan by a ford, on his way to Shechem (today's Nablus).

ABOVE: Jacob's Well in Nablus, said to be the site where Jacob camped and bought a plot of ground. According to John (4:12), Jacob dug a well here for himself, his children, and his flocks. According to Genesis (33:20), he erected an altar here and named it *El*, God of Israel.

OPPOSITE: On the highway between the twin mountains of Ebal and Gerizim—now the busy main street of the Arab town of Nablus—the famous biblical promise to Abraham, "Unto thy seed will I give this land" (Genesis 12:7), is said to have been given.

OVERLEAF: Samaria is the mountain region on the central plateau of the Holy Land between the Jordan valley in the east and the coastal plain in the west. When the united Hebrew kingdom broke up after the death of Solomon (ca. 930 B.C.), Judea became the southern and Samaria the northern kingdom. The northern kingdom lasted until 722 B.C., when it was vanquished by the Assyrians under Sargon and its population forcibly removed to the east (hence the "Ten Lost Tribes"). It is a prosperous agricultural region, rich in wheat, olives, and fruit, and is today inhabited mostly by Palestinian Arabs.

The Jordan River, the longest river in Israel, below the Sea of Galilee (*above*) and above the sea (*opposite*), feeds the lush, fertile plains of the Jordan valley (*overleaf*).

ABOVE: Belvoir castle was built by the Crusaders in 1168 some 1,640 feet above the Jordan rift valley to defend the eastern approaches to the highlands.

OPPOSITE: Hisham palace at Khirbet al Mafjar, just outside Jericho, an eighth-century Umayyad pleasure spot and royal hunting lodge, included a mosque, baths, colonnaded courts, mosaics, and ornamental pools. Unique among Moslem sites in Palestine in its spectacular extravagance and unorthodox figurative decoration, its construction has been attributed to Walid ibn Yazid, the caliph Hisham's nephew who was banished from court for drinking alcohol and wild living in general, and for preferring the company of actors and singers to that of pious scholars.

OVERLEAF: Another view of the Sea of Galilee. The sea, or lake really, is harp-shaped, hence its Hebrew name Kinneret (kinnor = harp). In the first century, the west side of the lake was lined with Jewish villages. In A.D. 20 Herod Antipas founded the city of Tiberias here. Under the Crusaders the entire area around the lake was taken by Tancred, who made himself Prince of Galilee in 1099. On a hill overlooking the lake, a few miles west of here, Saladin won the famous battle of Hittin that destroyed the Latin Kingdom of Jerusalem.

THESE PAGES AND OVERLEAF: The Negev (which means not "south" as in the English translation of the Bible but literally the "parched land") is a dry region, much of it desert, which extends from south of Beer Sheba down to the Red Sea and the Sinai. Its mineral resources were mined by the ancients but are not considered economically exploitable today.

ABOVE: Beer Sheba (literally, "Well of the Covenant," as in Genesis 21:32) was the southern limit of the Promised Land (from Dan to Beer Sheba) and a noted sanctuary at the time of the Patriarchs: "And Abraham planted a grove in Beer-sheba, and called there on the name of the Lord, the everlasting God" (Genesis 21:33). A small Arab town until 1948, it became a new city when Israel was established and today has a population of two hundred thousand inhabitants. Pictured is the campus of the new Ben Gurion University of the Negev.

OPPOSITE: Elath is Israel's southernmost city on the shores of the Red Sea. There was nothing here in 1948 when Israel was established. The two dozen tin huts that stood here in 1950 have since become a port city of some fifty thousand inhabitants and a major winter and summer resort.

THESE PAGES: Over 1,900 years ago a remarkable people, the Nabateans, lived in the Negev Desert and successfully harnessed the perennial rivers in the wilderness. They developed agriculture in the harsh environment and built great cities such as Avdath (*left*). Aerial surveys have shown that hundreds of thousands of acres of desert land had been under cultivation by the Nabateans to support their relatively dense population. Modern farming in this area, as in Sde Boker (*above*), while using the latest achievements of agrotechnology, reapplies some of the sophisticated techniques of utilizing run-off waters first developed centuries ago by the Nabateans.

OVERLEAF: The tomb of David Ben-Gurion, Israel's first prime minister (*bottom right*) at Sde Boker, the desert kibbutz he joined after his retirement.

The Dead Sea: its level fluctuates, but at its median (1,300 feet below sea level) it is the lowest point on earth. Fed by the Jordan at its northernmost point, the Dead Sea has no exit. Its water is lost mainly through evaporation in the great heat. The evaporation produces a concentrated accumulation of mineral salts, making the sea almost ten times denser than ordinary sea water. It is possible to sit in the water and read a newspaper without sinking. Its mineral salts (mostly potassium chloride) are extracted by a Jordanian plant on its eastern shore and by an Israeli plant on its southern shore. In the fourth century B.C., the Egyptians imported bitumen from the Dead Sea for embalming their dead. The curative and other properties of Dead Sea salts exercised the imagination of ancient writers, from Aristotle to Pliny, Strabo, and Tacitus.

The Dead Sea and the Jordan River Valley together form part of the so-called Afro-Asian Rift, which reaches down south through the Red Sea as far as Kenya. The legend of Sodom and Gomorrah, traditionally located here at the southern end of the Dead Sea (*opposite*), may echo the distant cataclysm which brought the Afro-Asian Rift into being long before historical times. Genesis 19:24–25 says that "the Lord rained upon Sodom and Gemorrah brimstone and fire. . . . And he overthrew those cities, and all the plain."

Rock and fortress of Masada: "Long ago we resolved never to be servants to the Romans nor to any other than God himself. . . . We were the first to revolt against them. I cannot but esteem it a favour that God has granted us that it is still in our power to die bravely and in a state of freedom, unlike others who were conquered unexpectedly. It is very plain that we shall be taken in a day's time; but it is still an eligible thing to die after a glorious manner together with our dearest friends. . . . Let us then save our wives before they are abused and our children before they have tasted of slavery; and after we have slain them let us bestow that glorious benefit upon one another mutually, and preserve ourselves in freedom as an excellent funeral monument for us" (Eleazar Ben Yair, zealots' general at Masada, quoted by Josephus Flavius in *Wars of the Jews*).